Sanjeev Kapoor's
KHAZANA

Vegetarian Cooking with Dahi

In association with Alyona Kapoor

Popular Prakashan
www.popularprakashan.com

Published by
POPULAR PRAKASHAN PVT. LTD.
301, Mahalaxmi Chambers
22, Bhulabhai Desai Road
Mumbai - 400 026
for Khana Khazana Publications Pvt. Ltd.

First Published 2010
First Reprint November 2012

(4123)
ISBN: 978-81-7991-375-8

Design: Anjali Sawant
Photography: Bharat Bhirangi

PRINTED IN INDIA
by HT Media Limited
B - 2, Sector - 63, Noida

AUTHOR'S NOTE

Nutritious dahi has been an integral part of the Indian meal for ages, due to its cooling and digestive qualities. Dahi has myriad health benefits, since it is packed with protein, vitamins and calcium. It strengthens the immune system.

Cooking with dahi is easy! Find out how, with my selection of Indian and international dishes. Try the cooling Chilled Cucumber and Buttermilk Soup, or the exotic Chilled Musk Melon Soup. Enjoy the chatpata Kachori Chaat, the delectable Dahi Papad ki Sabzi, or a light Beans with Tomato-Yogurt Sauce.

It's healthy and dahi-licious!

Happy cooking!

CONTENTS

BEVERAGES, SOUPS AND SALADS

SNACKS

MAIN COURSE

RICE AND KADHI

DESSERTS

MANGO LASSI

1 cup mango pulp

3 cups yogurt

¼ cup sugar

¼ cup Chocolate Sauce (page 95)

15-20 pistachios, blanched and slivered

Crushed ice

- In a blender, blend together the mango pulp and sugar. Add the yogurt and blend again. Add the crushed ice and blend to a smooth mixture.
- Pour the chocolate sauce into a squeezy bottle. Squeeze the sauce in a striped design along the inner sides of serving glasses. Pour the *lassi* into the glasses.
- Garnish with some more chocolate sauce, and top with pistachio slivers. Serve chilled.

KIWI VANILLA LASSI

2 medium kiwi fruits, peeled and chopped

2 scoops vanilla ice cream

3 cups yogurt, whisked

5 tablespoons sugar

Crushed ice, as required

- Set aside four teaspoons of the kiwi and combine the rest with the yogurt and the sugar in a blender, and blend till smooth.
- Add the vanilla ice cream and crushed ice and blend again for a minute.
- Pour the *lassi* into the individual tall glasses and serve garnished with the reserved kiwi.

LEMON BANANA LASSI

1 tablespoon lemon juice

3 medium bananas, sliced

2 cups yogurt

½ cup sugar

Ice cubes

- Whisk the yogurt in a blender. Add the bananas, lemon juice and sugar, and blend well.
- Add a few ice cubes to the *lassi* and blend again.
- Pour into the tall glasses and serve immediately.

VAGHARELI CHAAS

1¼ cups yogurt

1 teaspoon oil

¼ teaspoon cumin seeds

1 tablespoon ginger, chopped

2-3 green chillies, chopped

8-10 curry leaves

1 tablespoon chopped fresh coriander

1 tablespoon chopped fresh mint

Salt to taste

- Whisk the yogurt with three cups of water till smooth. Heat the oil in a non-stick pan and add the cumin seeds. When they change colour, add the ginger, green chillies and the curry leaves, and sauté.
- Add the seasoning to the yogurt and mix. Add the chopped coriander and the chopped mint. Mix well.
- Serve at room temperature.

CHILLED CUCUMBER AND BUTTERMILK SOUP

- 2 medium cucumbers, peeled, seeded and roughly chopped
- 2 cups buttermilk
- ½ inch ginger, roughly chopped
- 1 green chilli, seeded and chopped
- 2 teaspoons lemon juice
- A few sprigs of mint leaves
- Salt to taste
- ½ teaspoon pepper powder

- Reserve a few sprigs of mint leaves for garnishing, and finely chop the rest.
- Place the cucumbers, ginger, green chilli and lemon juice in a blender, and process till smooth.
- Stir in the buttermilk and the chopped mint. Season with salt and pepper powder.
- Garnish with the chopped mint and serve chilled.

Chef's Tip: Buttermilk should not have lumps. If you do not have buttermilk, you can mix equal quantities of yogurt and water, and whisk till smooth.

CHILLED MUSK MELON SOUP

1 (1 kilogram) musk melon, halved and seeded and cut into 1-inch pieces

1 inch ginger, roughly chopped

A few sprigs of mint leaves

¼ cup yogurt

3 tablespoons lemon juice

Salt to taste

¼ teaspoon pepper powder

2 cups crushed ice

- Reserve a few mint sprigs for garnishing.
- In a blender, purée the muskmelon, ginger and mint. Add the yogurt, lemon juice and crushed ice, blend for a few minutes more.
- Season with the salt and pepper powder.
- Serve chilled, garnished with a sprig of mint.

Chef's Tips: 1. Consistency of this soup is normally very thick, however if you prefer you may thin it down by adding half a cup of chilled milk.

2. Go easy on mint leaves as too much mint flavour and taste can be too over powering.

CURRIED CAULIFLOWER SOUP

1 medium cauliflower, separated into small florets

1 medium potato, cut into small pieces

1½ teaspoons oil

1 medium onion, finely chopped

½ inch ginger, finely chopped

4 garlic cloves, finely chopped

A few sprigs of fresh coriander, chopped

4 cups Vegetable Stock (page 95)

½ teaspoons cumin seeds

¼ teaspoons mustard seeds

½ teaspoons turmeric powder

2 teaspoons coriander powder

1 cup yogurt

½ cup milk

2 teaspoons gram flour

Salt to taste

- Soak the cauliflower and potato separately, in salted water.
- Heat one teaspoon oil in a thick-bottomed non-stick pan; add the chopped onion and sauté for two minutes. Add the chopped ginger and garlic, and sauté

for another two minutes. Drain and add the chopped potato. Drain and add the cauliflower and stir on high heat for three to four minutes.

- Stir in two cups of the vegetable stock and bring to a boil. Cover and simmer till the cauliflower and potato are cooked. Remove from the heat and cool the mixture. Purée the cauliflower and potato mixture in a blender.
- Heat half a teaspoon oil in a non-stick pan and add the cumin seeds and mustard seeds. When the mustard seeds start to splutter, add the cauliflower and potato purée along with the remaining vegetable stock. Mix well and cook on low heat. Add the turmeric powder and coriander powder, and mix well.
- Whisk the yogurt and milk in a bowl. Add the gram flour and continue to whisk till smooth. Stir the mixture into the soup and cook for a while. Season with salt if required.
- Serve hot, garnished with the chopped coriander.

Chef's Tip: A leftover dish made of potatoes and cauliflower can be puréed and used to make the soup.

BESAN CHEELA RAITA

¾ cup gram flour
2 cups thick yogurt, whisked
1 teaspoon red chilli powder
½ teaspoon cumin seeds
¼ teaspoon powdered mustard seeds
Salt to taste
A pinch of soda bicarbonate
1 teaspoon oil + for shallow-frying
1 teaspoon sugar
A pinch of asafoetida
1 tablespoon chopped coriander

- In a bowl, combine the gram flour, half the chilli powder, the cumin seeds, powdered mustard seeds and salt to taste. Add enough water to make a thick batter. Whisk thoroughly to remove lumps. Add the soda bicarbonate and whisk well.

- Heat a non-stick *tawa* and apply a little oil. Drop small spoonfuls of the gram flour batter on the *tawa* and shallow-fry the small *cheele* using more oil if needed. Fry till golden brown on both sides.

- Add half a cup of water to the yogurt and add the remaining chilli powder, the sugar and salt to taste. Add the *cheele* to the yogurt.
- Heat a teaspoon of oil in a small non-stick pan and add the remaining cumin seeds. When they begin to change colour, add the remaining powdered mustard seeds and asafoetida. Remove from heat immediately and pour over the yogurt.
- Serve at once, garnished with the chopped coriander.

VEGETABLE CRUDITÉS WITH GREEK YOGURT DIP

8-10 cherry tomatoes, halved

2 medium carrots, cut into fingers

1 medium white radish, cut into fingers

4 red radishes, quartered

2 medium cucumbers, cut into fingers

4 cups yogurt, drained

¼ cup fresh mint leaves

1 teaspoon lemon juice

¼ teaspoon white sesame seeds, toasted

4 garlic cloves, finely chopped

Salt to taste

8-10 iceberg lettuce leaves, soaked in chilled water

- Chop the mint leaves, reserving some for garnishing.
- In a bowl, combine the drained yogurt, chopped mint, lemon juice, sesame seeds and garlic. Add salt to taste and place in a refrigerator to chill.

- Just before serving, drain and arrange the lettuce leaves on a serving plate.
- Arrange the prepared vegetables on the leaves in an attractive design.
- Serve with the chilled dressing.

***Note:** To drain the yogurt, hang it in a piece of muslin, preferably in a refrigerator, till all the whey is drained away. You can use the whey in some other dish.*

LAUKI RAITA

200 grams bottle gourd, grated

2 cups yogurt

Salt to taste

½ tablespoon oil

½ teaspoon cumin seeds

½ teaspoon red chilli powder

A pinch of asafoetida

- Add the salt to the grated bottle gourd and set aside for half an hour. Squeeze out the water thoroughly.
- Whisk the yogurt in a bowl, add the grated bottle gourd and mix well.
- Heat the oil in a non-stick *kadai*. Add the cumin seeds and when they begin to change colour, add the chilli powder and asafoetida.
- Add the sizzling spices to the yogurt mixture and cover the bowl immediately. Leave to stand for three to four minutes.
- Stir to mix, adjust salt and serve chilled.

GRAPE AND WALNUT RAITA

25-30 green grapes, halved
¼ cup walnut kernels, chopped
2 cups yogurt
Salt to taste
1½ teaspoons sugar
½ teaspoon roasted cumin powder
2 tablespoons chopped fresh mint
A large pinch of red chilli powder

- Whisk the yogurt in a large bowl with salt, sugar and cumin powder.
- Add the grapes, walnuts and mint, and fold in gently. Place in a refrigerator to chill.
- Sprinkle chilli powder and serve.

CANAPÉS WITH CHOLE

16 ready-made canapés, fried

1½ cups yogurt, whisked and chilled

1 teaspoon red chilli powder

2 teaspoons roasted cumin powder

2 teaspoons *chaat masala*

¼ cup Green Chutney (page 32)

Chole

1 cup chickpeas, soaked

Salt to taste

2 teaspoons tea leaves

2 tablespoons ghee

2 medium onions, chopped

1 teaspoon ginger paste

1 teaspoon garlic paste

4 tablespoons *chole masala*

¾ cup fresh tomato purée

4 tablespoons chopped fresh coriander

- To make the *chole*, place the chickpeas with three cups of water and salt in a pressure cooker. Tie up the tea leaves in a piece of muslin to make a *potli*; add to the chickpeas. Close the lid and cook till the pressure is released five to six times (five to six whistles) or till the chickpeas are soft. Discard the *potli*. Drain and set aside. Reserve one-fourth cup of stock for cooking.

- Heat two tablespoons of the ghee in a non-stick *kadai*; add the onions and sauté over a low heat till light golden. Add the ginger paste and garlic paste, and sauté for half a minute.

- Add three tablespoons of the *chole masala* and continue to sauté for another minute. Add the tomato purée and cook over a low heat for two to three minutes.

- Add the boiled chickpeas and the reserved stock and simmer for five minutes, or till all the water is absorbed and the ghee rises to the surface.

- Sprinkle the remaining *chole masala* and chopped coriander, stir and cover immediately. Remove from the heat and keep warm. Place the canapés on individual serving plates. Fill each canapé with two to three tablespoons of the prepared *chole*.

- Pour some whisked yogurt over and sprinkle a little chilli powder, roasted cumin powder and *chaat masala*. Finally drizzle a little green chutney on each canapé and serve immediately.

ARBI TANDOORI

16 medium colocasia tubers

Salt to taste

¼ teaspoon turmeric powder

Melted butter, for basting

Marinade

½ cup drained (hung) yogurt

½ tablespoon gram flour

½ teaspoon dried fenugreek leaves, roasted and crushed

1 teaspoon ginger paste

1 teaspoon garlic paste

½ teaspoon red chilli powder

¾ tablespoon *tandoori masala* powder

¼ teaspoon *garam masala* powder

½ tablespoon lemon juice

Salt to taste

- Boil the colocasia in sufficient salted boiling water with the turmeric powder till almost done. Drain, refresh in cold water, peel and set aside.
- Mix together all the ingredients for the marinade in a large bowl.
- Flatten the boiled colocasia pieces lightly with your hand and add to the marinade. Mix lightly till evenly coated. Set aside to marinate for half an hour.
- Preheat the oven to 180°C/350°F/Gas Mark 4.
- Thread the colocasia tubers one by one onto a skewer and brush with some of the remaining marinade. Cook in the preheated oven for ten to fifteen minutes, basting occasionally with the melted butter.
- Remove from the skewers and serve hot.

STUFFED DAHI VADE

Vade

½ cup skinless split black gram

Salt to taste

A pinch of asafoetida

½ teaspoon cumin seeds

Oil for deep-frying

Stuffing

1 inch ginger, finely chopped

¾ tablespoon raisins

4-5 cashew nuts, crushed

1 green chilli, finely chopped

1 tablespoon chopped fresh coriander

Yogurt

2½ cups yogurt, whisked and chilled

Salt to taste

½ teaspoon rock salt

To Serve

½ cup Tamarind Chutney (page 95)

1 teaspoon red chilli powder

1 teaspoon roasted cumin powder

¼ cup chopped fresh coriander

- Soak the split black gram for three to four hours. Drain and grind, using very little water, to make a thick, coarse but fluffy batter. Add the salt, asafoetida and cumin seeds, and mix well.

- Mix together the ginger, raisins, cashew nuts, green chillies and chopped coriander in a bowl.

- Heat the oil in a non-stick *kadai*. Wet your hands and place a small portion of batter on one palm and pat lightly with wet fingers to flatten it. Place a little stuffing in the centre and bring the edges together to enclose the filling.

- Gently lower each *vada* into the hot oil and fry till golden brown. Drain and soak the *vade* in cold water. Mix together the yogurt, salt and rock salt.

- Squeeze out the *vade* and arrange on a serving dish. Spoon chilled yogurt over the *vade*; top with tamarind chutney and sprinkle red chilli powder, cumin powder and chopped coriander.

FARALI CHAAT

1 cup *farali chiwda*

500 grams purple yam, boiled and cut into small cubes

1½ cups yogurt, whisked and chilled

2 tablespoons pure ghee

1 teaspoon cumin seeds

3 green chillies, chopped

2 teaspoons red chilli powder

3 tablespoons chopped fresh coriander

Rock salt to taste

4 teaspoons Green Chutney (see below)

4 teaspoons Date and Tamarind Chutney (see below)

- Heat the ghee in a non-stick *kadai*; add the cumin seeds and sauté over a medium heat till they change colour.
- Add the green chillies and sauté for half a minute. Add the yam, chilli powder, chopped coriander and rock salt, and sauté for one minute, stirring and tossing continuously.

- Transfer the mixture to four serving plates. Pour three or four tablespoons of chilled yogurt over each portion.
- Drizzle one teaspoon each of green chutney and date and tamarind chutney, sprinkle one-fourth cup of *farali chiwda* and serve immediately.

- **Date and Tamarind Chutney**
  Wash, stone and chop 15-20 dates. Dry-roast 2 teaspoons cumin seeds and ¼ teaspoon fennel seeds. Cool and grind to a powder. Cook the dates, 1 cup tamarind pulp, cumin and fennel powder, ½ cup jaggery, 2 teaspoons red chilli powder, 1 teaspoon dried ginger powder, black salt, salt and four cups of water till thick.
- **Green Chutney**
  Grind together 1 cup fresh coriander, ½ cup fresh mint, 2-3 green chillies, black salt to taste, ¼ teaspoon sugar and 1 tablespoon lemon juice to a smooth paste using a little water if required.

INSTANT DAHI VADE

8 large *jeera* butter biscuits

4 cups thin buttermilk

2½ cups yogurt, whisked and chilled

½ teaspoon rock salt

1 teaspoon red chilli powder

1 teaspoon roasted cumin powder

½ cup Date and Tamarind Chutney (page 32)

¼ cup chopped fresh coriander

- Soak the *jeera* biscuits in buttermilk for eight to ten minutes till soft. Drain, squeeze lightly between your palms and set aside. Alternatively, soak the biscuits in four cups of warm water for four or five minutes and drain.

- Place the two soaked biscuits in each serving bowl, and pour the chilled yogurt over the biscuits.

- Serve, garnished with rock salt, chilli powder, cumin powder, date and tamarind chutney and chopped coriander.

KASOORI PANEER TIKKA

- 2 tablespoons dried fenugreek leaves, roasted and crushed
- 250 grams cottage cheese, cut into 1½-inch pieces
- 1 medium green capsicum, cut into 1½-inch pieces
- 1 medium onion, cut into 1½-inch cubes
- 1 medium tomato, seeded, and cut into 1½-inch pieces
- 1 cup yogurt
- 2 tablespoons Green Chutney (page 32)
- 1 teaspoon green chilli paste
- 1 teaspoon ginger paste
- 1 teaspoon garlic paste
- ¼ teaspoon turmeric powder
- 1 teaspoon *garam masala* powder
- 1 teaspoon *chaat masala*
- 2 tablespoons roasted *chana dal* powder
- ¼ cup fresh cream
- Salt to taste
- 2 tablespoons mustard oil
- 2 tablespoons oil
- 2 tablespoons lemon juice

- Mix together the yogurt, green chutney, green chilli paste, ginger paste, garlic paste, turmeric powder, *garam masala* powder, half a teaspoon of *chaat masala*, crushed fenugreek leaves, roasted *chana dal* powder, cream and salt in a bowl. Add the cottage cheese cubes and marinate for about fifteen minutes.
- Heat the mustard oil in a non-stick pan to smoking point and set aside to cool. When completely cold, stir the oil into the cottage cheese cubes.
- Soak a few wooden skewers in water for fifteen minutes.
- Thread the capsicum, cottage cheese, tomato and onion cubes one after the other onto the skewers.
- Heat the oil in a non-stick grill pan, on medium heat, turning the skewers a few times so that the *tikka* cook on all sides.
- Arrange the *tikka* on a plate, sprinkle with the remaining *chaat masala* and lemon juice, and serve hot.

KACHORI CHAAT

1 cup refined flour

¼ teaspoon carom seeds

¼ teaspoon salt

A pinch of soda bicarbonate

2 tablespoons pure ghee

Oil for deep-frying

Filling

½ cup shelled green peas, lightly crushed

½ tablespoon oil

A pinch of asafoetida

¼ teaspoon cumin seeds

½ inch ginger, chopped

2 green chillies, chopped

Salt to taste

¼ teaspoon *garam masala* powder

2 tablespoons grated coconut

2 tablespoons roasted peanuts, crushed

Topping

2 cups yogurt, whisked and chilled

1 teaspoon red chilli powder

2 teaspoons roasted cumin powder

4 teaspoons Green Chutney (page 32)

4 teaspoons Date and Tamarind Chutney (page 32)

- For the filling, heat the oil in a non-stick pan; add the asafoetida and cumin seeds. When the cumin seeds begin to change colour, add the ginger, green chillies, green peas and salt. Mix and cook for two or three minutes. Remove from the heat and stir in the *garam masala* powder. Set aside to cool. When completely cold, add the coconut and peanuts, and mix well.
- For the *kachori*, mix together the refined flour, carom seeds, salt, soda bicarbonate and pure ghee in a bowl. Add enough cold water and knead into a stiff dough.
- Divide the dough into eight equal portions. Roll out each portion and press to make round *puri*. Stuff each *puri* with the stuffing and shape into a *kachori*.
- Heat plenty of oil in a non-stick *kadai* and deep-fry the *kachori* in moderately hot oil till crisp and golden. Drain on absorbent paper.
- To serve, lightly crush two to three *kachori* and place them in individual serving bowls. Pour some yogurt over, sprinkle the chilli powder and cumin powder, drizzle both the chutneys and serve immediately.

SURKH TANDOORI ALOO

20 baby potatoes
2 tablespoons oil + for deep-frying
1½ cup drained (hung) yogurt
1 tablespoon ginger-garlic paste
2 teaspoons Kashmiri red chilli paste
Salt to taste
¼ teaspoon carom seed powder
1 teaspoon *garam masala* powder
4 tablespoons roasted gram flour
2 tablespoons lemon juice

- Heat sufficient oil in a non-stick *kadai* and deep-fry the potatoes till they are half-cooked. Drain on absorbent paper and set aside.
- Place the yogurt in a bowl. Add the ginger-garlic paste, chilli paste, salt, carom seed powder, *garam masala* powder, roasted gram flour, lemon juice and two tablespoons of oil, and mix well.
- Add the fried potatoes to the marinade and mix gently. Set aside in a refrigerator to marinate for about an hour.

- Thread the potatoes a little apart onto skewers and roast in a *tandoor*, or cook in an oven at 200°C/400°F/ Gas Mark 6 for six to eight minutes, or till golden brown and crisp.
- Serve hot with onion *lachcha*.

ALOO KA RASSAWALA SHAAK

4 medium boiled potatoes, cut into ½-inch pieces

1 cup yogurt

1 tablespoon gram flour

Salt to taste

¼ teaspoon turmeric powder

1 tablespoon pure ghee

½ teaspoon cumin seeds

A pinch of asafoetida

7-8 curry leaves

½ inch ginger, chopped

2 green chillies, chopped

¼ teaspoon red chilli powder

½ teaspoon *garam masala* powder

- Whisk the yogurt with the gram flour, salt and turmeric powder. Add three-fourth cup of water and mix well.
- Heat the ghee in a non-stick pan. Add the cumin seeds and when they begin to change colour, add the asafoetida, curry leaves, ginger and green chillies. Sauté for a minute.

- Add the chilli powder and yogurt mixture, and mix well.
- Add the potatoes and cook, stirring continuously, till the mixture comes to a boil. Lower the heat and simmer for five to six minutes.
- Sprinkle with the *garam masala* powder and serve hot.

ARBI KA KHATTA SHAAK

250 grams colocasia tubers, boiled, peeled and sliced

1 cup yogurt

2 teaspoons gram flour

1 teaspoon coriander powder

1 teaspoon red chilli powder

1 teaspoon dried mango powder

½ teaspoon *garam masala* powder

Salt to taste

1½ tablespoons ghee

½ teaspoon carom seeds

A pinch of asafoetida

1 teaspoon ginger paste

2 teaspoons garlic paste

2 tablespoons chopped fresh coriander

- Whisk together the yogurt, gram flour, coriander powder, chilli powder, dried mango powder, *garam masala* powder and salt.
- Heat the ghee in a non-stick pan; add the carom seeds and asafoetida, and sauté for ten seconds.

- Add the sliced colocasia and sauté on medium heat till light brown.
- Add the ginger and garlic pastes, and sauté for two minutes.
- Add the yogurt mixture and cook on medium heat till most of the moisture dries up and the gravy thickens.
- Garnish with the chopped coriander and serve hot.

DAHI PAPAD KI SABZI

1½ cups sour yogurt

3 *Bikaneri moong papad*

¾ tablespoon gram flour

½ teaspoon turmeric powder

¾ teaspoon red chilli powder

Salt to taste

1½ tablespoons pure ghee

1 teaspoon cumin seeds

1½ teaspoons coriander powder

½ teaspoon asafoetida

2 dried red chillies, broken into large bits

¾ cup *boondi*

1 tablespoon chopped fresh coriander

½ teaspoon *garam masala* powder

- In a large bowl, combine the yogurt, gram flour, turmeric powder, chilli powder and salt. Add two cups of water and mix well. Strain and set aside.

- Heat the ghee in a non-stick *kadai* and add the cumin seeds. When they change colour, add the coriander powder and sauté for one minute.

- Add the asafoetida and red chillies, and sauté for half a minute. Add the yogurt mixture and adjust the seasoning.
- Stir continuously till the mixture comes to a boil. Lower the heat and simmer for two minutes.
- Heat a non-stick *tawa* and roast the *papad* on both sides. Break them roughly into two-inch pieces.
- Add the *papad* and *boondi* to the simmering yogurt mixture and cook for two or three minutes.
- Garnish with the chopped coriander and *garam masala* powder. Serve hot.

BEANS WITH TOMATO-YOGURT SAUCE

20-25 French beans, cut into 3-inch pieces

3 medium tomatoes, blanched, seeded and chopped

1½ cup yogurt

Salt to taste

3 medium spring onions

1 tablespoon maize flour

1 inch ginger

5 garlic cloves

1 teaspoon oil

2 dried red chillies, crushed

- Blanch the French beans in boiling salted water until cooked. Strain, and reserve the liquid to use as stock. Refresh the beans in cold water and drain.
- Finely chop the spring onion bulbs, reserving the spring onion greens.
- Slit the cooked beans into two and tie them up in bundles with the spring onion greens.

- For the tomato-yogurt sauce, whisk together the yogurt and maize flour. Grind together the ginger and garlic to a fine paste.
- Heat the oil in a non-stick pan; add the chopped onion and cook until translucent.
- Add the ginger-garlic paste and stir-fry for a few seconds. Add the tomatoes and cook for two to three minutes.
- Lower the heat and add the yogurt-maize flour mixture and salt to taste. Cook, stirring continuously till it thickens.
- To serve, warm the cooked beans, in a microwave oven for one minute on HIGH (100%). Alternatively, dip them in boiling hot water or stock. Arrange on a serving dish and drizzle the sauce on top.
- Sprinkle the crushed chillies and serve hot.

BHARWAN GATTE

- 2½ cups gram flour
- 2 cups yogurt, whisked
- 1½ teaspoons red chilli powder
- ½ teaspoon turmeric powder
- 1 teaspoon ginger paste
- Salt to taste
- ¼ teaspoon soda bicarbonate
- ½ cup grated cottage cheese
- ½ cup grated *khoya/mawa*
- 4 green chillies, chopped
- 2 tablespoons oil
- 1 teaspoon cumin seeds
- ¼ teaspoon fenugreek seeds
- 8-10 black peppercorns
- 3 dried red chillies, broken into large bits
- A pinch of asafoetida
- ½ teaspoon *garam masala* powder
- 2 tablespoons chopped fresh coriander

- Whisk the yogurt with two cups of water, two tablespoons of gram flour, the chilli powder and turmeric powder.
- Mix the remaining gram flour with the ginger paste, salt and soda bicarbonate. Add enough water and knead well to make a stiff dough. Set aside for five minutes.
- In a bowl, mix together the grated cottage cheese, *khoya*, half the green chillies and salt. Divide into sixteen equal portions.
- Divide the gram flour dough into sixteen equal portions. Flatten each

portion and stuff it with one portion of the cottage cheese-*khoya* mixture. Shape into cylinders.

- Cook the stuffed *gatte* in boiling water for ten to fifteen minutes. Drain and cut into one-inch pieces.
- Heat the oil in a non-stick *kadai*; add the cumin seeds and stir-fry till they change colour. Add the fenugreek seeds, peppercorns, red chillies, remaining green chillies and asafoetida, and sauté for a minute.
- Add the whisked yogurt, and cook, stirring continuously, for three to four minutes, until the gravy thickens slightly. Add the *garam masala* powder, and adjust the seasoning. Add water if required.
- Add the cooked *gatte* to the gravy and continue cooking till the gravy thickens.
- Garnish with the chopped coriander and serve hot.

DAHIWALE AMRUD

4 medium guavas, seeded and cut into small pieces

½ cup yogurt

½ tablespoon coriander powder

¼ teaspoon red chilli powder

¼ teaspoon turmeric powder

1 teaspoon dried mango powder

1 tablespoon ghee

2 green chillies, chopped

½ teaspoon cumin seeds

½ teaspoon fennel seeds

¼ teaspoon asafoetida

1 medium tomato, chopped

Salt to taste

¼ teaspoon *garam masala* powder

½ teaspoon sugar

- Whisk the yogurt with all the powdered spices, except the *garam masala* powder.
- Heat the ghee in a non-stick *kadai*; add the green chillies, cumin seeds, fennel seeds and asafoetida, and stir to mix.

- Cut the cottage cheese into half inch wide and one inch long pieces. Boil the onions in a quarter cup of water. Drain and set aside to cool. Grind the onions to a fine paste.

- Heat the oil in a non-stick pan on medium heat. Add the cloves, cinnamon and bay leaf, and sauté till fragrant. Add the chillies and boiled onion paste, and reduce the heat. Sauté taking care that the onions do not get coloured. Add the ginger paste and garlic paste, and continue to sauté for half a minute.

- Add the tomato purée and sauté till the oil separates. Add the chilli, coriander, turmeric and black pepper powders, and sauté for a minute.

- Add the cashew nut paste and sauté for another two minutes. Stir in the cream, saffron, *garam masala* powder, salt and one cup of water. Stir well and bring to a boil. Simmer for three minutes.

- Add the cottage cheese and stir gently. Sprinkle with the cardamom powder and serve hot.

KER SANGRI

½ cup desert berries	2 teaspoons ginger paste
1 cup dried desert beans	½ teaspoon turmeric powder
1 cup + 4 teaspoons yogurt, beaten	1 teaspoon red chilli powder
Salt to taste	1 teaspoon coriander powder
2 tablespoons oil	5-6 pieces of dried mango
1 teaspoon cumin seeds	1 teaspoon dried mango powder
5-6 dried red chillies, broken into large bits	1 tablespoon chopped fresh coriander

- Soak the berries and dried beans in one cup of beaten yogurt overnight. Remove from the yogurt and wash under running water.
- Boil them for fifteen to twenty minutes in two cups of water with salt. Drain.

- Heat the oil in a non-stick *kadai*; add the cumin seeds, red chillies and ginger paste, and sauté till the cumin seeds change colour.

- Add a little water, turmeric powder, chilli powder and coriander powder, and stir. Add the dried mango pieces and four teaspoons of yogurt, and mix well.

- Add the berries and beans to the pan, and mix. Add the salt, dried mango powder and chopped coriander, and mix well.

- Serve hot.

MICROWAVED VEGETABLE KORMA

1 medium potato, peeled and cut into ½-inch cubes

½ medium cauliflower, separated into florets

1 medium carrot, cut into ½-inch cubes

½ cup shelled green peas

10-15 French beans, cut into ½-inch pieces

1 medium green capsicum, cut into ½-inch pieces

2 tablespoons oil

2 medium onions, grated

¼ teaspoon turmeric powder

½ cup yogurt

Salt to taste

1 tablespoon *garam masala* powder

¼ cup chopped fresh coriander

Masala

2 tablespoons oil

½ cup grated fresh coconut

8 garlic cloves, roughly chopped

1 inch ginger, roughly chopped

4 green chillies, coarsely chopped

2 tablespoons coriander seeds

1 teaspoon cumin seeds

2 tablespoons poppy seeds

- For the *masala*, place the oil and the ingredients in a microwave-safe bowl. Cook, uncovered, on HIGH (100%) for four minutes till lightly browned. Cool and grind to a paste with one-fourth cup of water.
- Place the oil into a microwave-safe bowl with the *masala*, onions and turmeric powder. Cook, uncovered, on HIGH (100%) for six minutes.
- Stir in the vegetables, yogurt, salt and one cup of water and continue cooking, covered, for ten minutes on HIGH (100%).
- Sprinkle with the *garam masala* powder, stir well and serve hot, garnished with chopped coriander.

MICROWAVED DAHIWALE ALOO

1 cup yogurt
4 medium potatoes
1 tablespoon oil
1 tablespoon gram flour
A pinch of asafoetida
½ teaspoon cumin seeds
½ inch ginger, chopped
Salt to taste
1 teaspoon red chilli powder
1 teaspoon *garam masala* powder
½ teaspoon coriander powder
¼ teaspoon turmeric powder
2-3 green chillies, chopped
1 tablespoon fresh coriander, chopped

- Rub half a tablespoon of the oil over the potatoes and arrange on a microwave-safe plate. Cook, uncovered, on HIGH (100%) for ten minutes. Cool, peel and cut into one-inch cubes.
- Whisk together the yogurt and gram flour until smooth.

- Place the remaining oil in a microwave-safe bowl together with the asafoetida, cumin seeds and ginger. Cook, uncovered, on HIGH (100%) for one minute.
- Stir in the yogurt mixture, potatoes, salt, chilli powder, *garam masala* powder, coriander powder, turmeric powder and green chillies.
- Cook, uncovered, on HIGH (100%) for five minutes. Leave to stand for five minutes. Serve hot, garnished with chopped coriander.

BAKALA BHAAT

1½ cups *kolam* rice
1 cup yogurt
½ cup milk
Salt to taste
1 tablespoon oil
1 teaspoon mustard seeds
¼ teaspoon asafoetida
1 dried red chilli, broken into bits
8-10 curry leaves
1 inch ginger, chopped
4 green chillies, chopped
¼ cup fresh cream
1 medium cucumber, seeded and grated
1 medium carrot, grated

- Boil the rice in four and a half cups of water and overcook it slightly. Drain well and set aside to cool. When it reaches room temperature, add the milk and salt to taste.
- Heat the oil in a small non-stick pan; add the mustard seeds, asafoetida, red chilli and curry leaves. When the seeds begin to splutter, add the ginger and green chillies, and sauté for half a minute. Add to the rice.
- Stir in the yogurt and cream, and chill in a refrigerator.
- Squeeze out the excess water from the cucumber. Garnish the rice with the cucumber and carrot, and serve.

PUDINA PANEER PULAO

1¾ cups Basmati rice

½ cup roughly chopped fresh mint

100 grams cottage cheese, cut into 1-inch cubes

2 green chillies, roughly chopped

1½ inches ginger, roughly chopped

¾ cup yogurt, whisked

2 tablespoons ghee

2 bay leaves

4-6 green cardamoms

4-6 cloves

2-3 black cardamoms

8-10 black peppercorns

Salt to taste

- Soak the rice in three cups of water for half an hour and drain.
- Grind the mint leaves, green chillies, ginger and yogurt into a smooth chutney.
- Heat the ghee in a thick-bottomed non-stick pan. Add the bay leaves, green cardamoms, cloves, black cardamoms and peppercorns. When they begin to sizzle, add the mint chutney and cook for two to three minutes.

- Add two and three-fourth cups of water and bring to a boil. Stir in salt to taste.
- Add the drained rice and bring to a boil. Cover the pan and cook over low heat for about eight to ten minutes, or till the rice is completely cooked.
- Gently stir in the cottage cheese and serve hot.

KATHAL KI BIRYANI

900 grams unripe green jackfruit, sliced and cut into 1½-inch cubes

1½ cups Basmati rice, soaked

Salt to taste

4 green cardamoms

3 black cardamoms

3 cloves

2 one-inch cinnamon sticks

5-6 saffron threads

2 tablespoons lukewarm milk

Oil for deep-frying

4 medium onions, thinly sliced

4 tablespoons pure ghee

½ teaspoon caraway seeds

1 tablespoon ginger paste

1 tablespoon garlic paste

1 teaspoon turmeric powder

1 teaspoon cumin powder

2 teaspoons coriander powder

3 teaspoons red chilli powder

3 medium tomatoes, chopped

1½ cups yogurt, whisked

½ cup chopped fresh coriander

1 teaspoon *garam masala* powder

¼ cup fresh mint, roughly torn

1 tablespoon screwpine water

AAMRAS KI KADHI

¾ cup unripe green mango pulp

¾ cup ripe mango pulp

2 tablespoons gram flour

Salt to taste

¾ cup buttermilk

1 tablespoon oil

A pinch of asafoetida

½ teaspoon mustard seeds

¼ teaspoon fenugreek seeds

6-8 curry leaves

2 green chillies, slit

½ cup *boondi*

- Mix together the unripe and ripe mango pulp, the gram flour and salt till smooth. Stir in the buttermilk.
- Heat the oil in a deep non-stick pan; add the asafoetida, mustard seeds and fenugreek seeds, and sauté till the mustard seeds begin to splutter. Add the curry leaves and green chillies, and sauté for two minutes.
- Stir in the mango mixture. Add one and a half cups of water and bring to a boil. Lower the heat and simmer for ten to fifteen minutes.
- Add the *boondi* and simmer for five more minutes. Serve hot.

ARBI KI KADHI

250 grams colocasia, boiled, peeled and cut into ½-inch thick slices

1 tablespoon oil + for deep-frying

¼ cup water chestnut flour

1½ cups sour yogurt

Rock salt to taste

1 teaspoon red chilli powder

½ teaspoon turmeric powder

½ teaspoon cumin seeds

2-3 dried red chillies, broken into large bits

1 tablespoon chopped fresh coriander

- Heat sufficient oil in a non-stick *kadai* and deep-fry the colocasia till golden brown. Drain on absorbent paper.
- Whisk the water chestnut flour into the yogurt till smooth. Add the rock salt, chilli powder and turmeric powder, and mix again. Add two cups of water and whisk well.
- Heat one tablespoon of the oil in a deep non-stick pan; add the cumin seeds and red chillies. When the cumin seeds begin to change colour, stir in the

yogurt mixture. Cook for five minutes, stirring continuously.

- Add the fried colocasia and mix. Continue cooking for five more minutes or till you get the desired consistency.
- Garnish with the chopped coriander and serve hot.

Chef's Tip: You can also make *aloo ki kadhi* by substituting potatoes for the colocasia.

BHINDA NI KADHI

15 ladies' fingers, cut into ½-inch pieces
2 cups sour yogurt
2 tablespoons oil
4 tablespoons gram flour
½ teaspoon turmeric powder
1 teaspoon red chilli powder
Salt to taste
¾ teaspoon mustard seeds
½ teaspoon fenugreek seeds
5 garlic cloves, sliced
1 inch ginger, cut into thin strips
2 green chillies, chopped
¼ teaspoon asafoetida
2 tablespoons chopped fresh coriander

- Heat one tablespoon of the oil in a non-stick pan; add the ladies' fingers and sauté till lightly browned.
- Whisk together the yogurt, gram flour, turmeric powder, chilli powder and salt till smooth. Add four cups of water and whisk again.
- Heat the remaining oil in a non-stick *kadai*; add the mustard seeds and fenugreek seeds. When they begin to splutter, add the garlic, ginger, green chillies and asafoetida, and sauté for half a minute.
- Add the yogurt mixture and bring to a boil. Lower the heat and cook, stirring continuously, till quite thick.
- Add the fried ladies' fingers and simmer for two or three minutes.
- Garnish with chopped coriander and serve hot.

VRAT KI KADHI

1¾ cups yogurt

2 tablespoons water chestnut flour

¼ teaspoon rock salt

1 teaspoon red chilli powder

¼ teaspoon cinnamon powder

2 tablespoons pure ghee

1 teaspoon cumin seeds

3 dried red chillies, broken into two pieces

10-12 curry leaves

½ teaspoon sugar

Salt to taste

1 tablespoon chopped fresh coriander

- Whisk together the yogurt, water chestnut flour, rock salt, chilli powder and cinnamon powder. Add four cups of water and mix well.
- Heat the ghee in a non-stick *kadai*; add the cumin seeds, red chillies and curry leaves. Sauté till the cumin seeds begin to splutter.
- Add the yogurt mixture and cook till the *kadhi* thickens slightly. Stir in the sugar and salt. Cook over a low heat for two minutes.
- Garnish with the chopped coriander and serve hot.

MAHARASHTRIAN KADHI

4 tablespoons gram flour
3 cups yogurt
Salt to taste
1 teaspoon turmeric powder
1 tablespoon oil
½ teaspoon mustard seeds
2 teaspoons ginger paste
1 teaspoon garlic paste
2 green chillies, slit
A pinch of asafoetida
4-6 curry leaves
2 tablespoons chopped fresh coriander

- Mix together the gram flour and yogurt thoroughly, in a deep non-stick pan. Add two cups of water, salt to taste and turmeric powder. Cook over a low heat stirring continuously.
- Heat the oil in a separate non-stick pan and add the mustard seeds. When they begin to splutter add the ginger paste, garlic paste, green chillies, asafoetida and curry leaves. Cook for one minute and pour the sizzling spices into the *kadhi*.
- Mix well and cook, stirring continuously, over a low heat until the *kadhi* has thickened slightly. Remove from heat and serve, garnished with chopped coriander.

PINEAPPLE YOGURT FOOL

½ medium pineapple, cut into small cubes

½ cup drained (hung) yogurt

½ cup sugar

1 inch cinnamon

- Mix together the pineapple, sugar and cinnamon in a non-stick pan and cook on low heat for thirty minutes. Set aside to cool.
- Remove the pineapple pieces and mix them with the yogurt. Process in a blender till smooth. Place in a refrigerator to chill.
- Serve chilled.

STRAWBERRY YOGURT

10-12 strawberries, chopped

2 cups thick yogurt

2 tablespoons powdered sugar

2 scoops vanilla ice cream

- Tie up the yogurt in a piece of muslin and hang over a bowl, preferably in a refrigerator, to drain.
- Mix together the drained yogurt, sugar and ice cream.
- Reserve two tablespoons of the chopped strawberries and add the rest to the yogurt mixture and process in a blender.
- Spoon into four bowls and place in a refrigerator to chill. Sprinkle the reserved strawberries on top and serve.

SHRIKHAND BISCUIT PUDDING

4 cups *kesari shrikhand*

20 sweet biscuits such as glucose biscuits

20 chocolate cream wafer biscuits

4 tablespoons butter, melted

2 medium ripe mangoes, chopped

1 kiwi fruit, sliced

Glazed cherries, to decorate

- Grease the base of an eight-inch springform cake tin with a little melted butter.
- Crush the sweet biscuits in a blender. Transfer to a bowl, add the melted butter and mix.
- Spread the mixture on the greased base of the cake tin and press down lightly.
- Arrange the chocolate wafer biscuits along the sides of the cake tin.
- Add the mangoes to the *shrikhand* and mix well.
- Pour the mango *shrikhand* over the biscuit layer and arrange the kiwi slices around the outer edge.
- Arrange the cherries in the middle and chill till set.
- Remove the pudding from the tin and serve.

YOGURT AND CHICKOO ICE CREAM

1 cup drained (hung) yogurt

6 medium *chickoo*, peeled and seeded

¼ cup powdered sugar

3 tablespoons honey

½ cup condensed milk

8-10 walnut kernels, crushed

- Place the *chickoo* in a processor, and process till crushed.
- Add the hung yogurt, powdered sugar and mix. Add the honey and process again.
- Add the condensed milk and mix. Finally add the crushed walnuts and mix.
- Transfer the mixture into an ice-cream tin and level the top.
- Place the tin in the deep freezer to set.
- Serve in scoops or slices when firmly set.

ANNEXURE

- **Chocolate Sauce**

  In a pan, mix together 2 cups milk and 4 tablespoons cocoa powder. Bring the mixture to a boil. Cook till it thickens. Add ½ cup sugar, and continue to cook for three to four minutes, stirring continuously. Add ¼ cup frozen butter, cut into ½-inch pieces and stir till melted and incorporated into the sauce. Serve warm.

- **Mint Chutney**

  Grind together 5 cups mint leaves, 3 cups coriander leaves, 10 green chillies, 3 onions, and 3 inches of ginger to a fine paste, adding a little water if required. Stir in 1 tablespoon lemon juice, salt and pomegranate seed powder to taste.

- **Tamarind Chutney**

  Soak 1 cup tamarind in two cups of warm water for half an hour. Squeeze out pulp and strain. Cook with 1¼ cups jaggery, and 1 inch cinnamon for fifteen minutes. Stir in 2 tablespoons raisins, salt, ¼ teaspoon black salt, 1 teaspoon red chilli powder, 1 teaspoon roasted cumin powder and 1½ teaspoons dried ginger powder. Cook for a while.

- **Vegetable Stock**

  Peel, wash and chop 1 onion, ½ medium carrot, 2-3 inch celery stalk and 2-3 garlic cloves. Place in a pan with 1 bay leaf, 5-6 peppercorns, 2-3 cloves and 5 cups of water and bring to a boil. Lower heat and simmer for 15 minutes and strain. Cool and store in a refrigerator till further use.

GLOSSARY

ENGLISH	HINDI
Berries	Ker
Black cardamoms	Badi elaichi
Black peppercorns	Kali mirch
Bottle gourd	Lauki
Capsicum	Shimla mirch
Caraway seeds	Shahi jeera
Carom seeds	Ajwain
Chickpeas	Kabuli chana
Cinnamon	Dalchini
Cloves	Laung
Colocasia	Arbi
Cottage cheese	Paneer
Cumin seeds	Jeera
Dried desert beans	Sangri
Dried fenugreek leaves	Kasoori methi
Dried mango powder	Amchur
Fennel seeds	Saunf
Fenugreek seeds	Methi dana

ENGLISH	HINDI
Fresh green pigeon peas	Tuvar ke taaze phalliyan
Gram, black skinless split	Dhuli urad dal
Guavas	Amrud
Jackfruit	Kathal
Musk melon	Kharbooj
Pistachio	Pista
Radish	Mooli
Roasted chana dal	Daalia
Rock salt	Sendha namak
Saffron	Kesar
Sesame seeds	Til
Turmeric powder	Haldi
Walnuts	Akhrot
Water chestnut	Singhara
Yam	Zamikand/suran
Yogurt	Dahi